Brown Bears

by Marcia S. Freeman

Consulting Editor:
Gail Saunders-Smith, Ph.D.

Consultant:
Don Middleton, Member
International Association for
Bear Research and Management

Pebble Books

an imprint of Capstone Press
Mankato, Minnesota

Pebble Books are published by Capstone Press
818 North Willow Street, Mankato, Minnesota 56001
http://www.capstone-press.com

Library of Congress Cataloging-in-Publication Data
Freeman, Marcia S. (Marcia Sheehan), 1937–
    Brown bears/by Marcia S. Freeman.
        p. cm.—(Bears)
    Includes bibliographical references and index.
    Summary: Simple text and photographs present the appearance, food, and behavior of the
brown bear.
    ISBN 0-7368-0097-2
    1. Brown bear—Juvenile literature. [1. Brown bear. 2. Bears.] I. Title. II. Series.
QL737.C27F727 1999
599.784—dc21   98-4216
                                                                   CIP
                                                                   AC

Note to Parents and Teachers

Books in this series may be used together in comparative activities to investigate
different types of bears. The series supports the national science education
standards for units on the diversity and unity of animal life. This book describes
and illustrates the appearance and activities of the brown bear. The photographs
support early readers in understanding the text. The sentence structures offer
subtle challenges. This book introduces early readers to vocabulary used in this
subject area. The vocabulary is defined in the Words to Know section. Early
readers may need assistance in reading some words and in using the Table of
Contents, Words to Know, Read More, Internet Sites, and Index/Word List
sections of the book.

Table of Contents

4

Brown bears have
brown or black fur.

Brown bears have
sharp claws.

Brown bears have
a shoulder hump.

Brown bears eat fish.

Brown bears eat grass.

14

Brown bears eat roots.

Brown bears find
dens during autumn.

Brown bears hibernate during winter.

Brown bears care
for their cubs.

Words to Know

berry—a small fruit found on bushes or trees

claw—a hard, curved nail on the foot of an animal

cub—a young bear

den—the home of an animal

fish—an animal that lives in water and has scales, fins, and gills

fur—the hairy coat of an animal

grass—a green plant with long, thin leaves that grows wild

hibernate—to spend the winter in a deep sleep

hump—a large lump that sticks out

paw—the foot of an animal; animals with paws have four feet.

root—the part of a plant that is underground

Read More

Down, Mike. *Bear.* Life Story. Mahwah, N.J.: Troll Associates, 1994.

Helmer, Diana Star. *Brown Bears.* Bears of the World. New York: PowerKids Press, 1997.

Holmes, Kevin J. *Bears.* Animals. Mankato, Minn.: Bridgestone Books, 1998.

Robinson, Claire. *Bears.* In the Wild. Crystal Lake, Ill.: Heinemann Library, 1997.

Internet Sites

The Bear Den—Brown Bear
http://www.bearden.org/brnbear.html

Brown and Grizzly Bears
http://www.nature-net.com/bears/brown.html

North American Bear Society
http://www.nonprofitnet.com/nabs/

Index/Word List

Word Count: **45**

Early-Intervention Level: **5**

Editorial Credits

Michelle L. Norstad, editor; Clay Schotzko/Icon Productions, cover designer; Sheri Gosewisch, photo researcher

Photo Credits

Animals Animals/Stouffer Prod., 16, 18

David Macias, 4, 12

GeoIMAGERY/Preston J. Garrison, cover

Lynn M. Stone, 8, 10

Photo Network/Mark Newman, 20

Root Resources/Alan G. Nelson, 6

Unicorn Stock Photos/Doug Adams, 14

Visuals Unlimited/Patrick J. Endres, 1